AMBERS TO BLUES

A COLLECTION OF POEMS THAT PORTRAYS THE DIFFERENT SHADES OF LIFE

RAASHI DHARIWAL

ISBN 979-888591185-6

Contents

Contents

Acknowledgements

Thank you to my beautiful audience, reading my debut book. I wish you have the best experience while reading the poems. In light of this book, I would like to extend my heartiest gratitude to the people who have supported me throughout the journey; my family, my extended family, or my friends, and to all those people who have encouraged me and had faith all along.

Thank you: R

Introduction

Life is a journey that is to be enjoyed and explored. This book consists of an assorted collection of poetry that depicts the same. For most people, their journeys begin on a joyful note, their childhoods. Cheerful friendships, naughty mischiefs, and making happy memories, all these things make their starts worth remembering. After a person grows older, the age of Romance begins. Love isn't easy, sometimes it's unrequited and on the other filled with ups and downs. But in the end, what's yours always finds you.

Just like the seasons keep changing, even life. There are social issues, there are insecurities. After a certain period when a person has travelled quite far in this journey, he wishes to take a pause and find pleasure in the beautiful nature around. There are times when this journey gets hard and all he wishes for is, it to end. But on the other hand, there are some happy times and joyful little nuances, which makes everything worth it.

Introduction

1. Childhood

-A nostalgic tour back
to the simpler times

How beautiful it looks,
When a bud blossoms into a flower.
Reminds me of my childhood days,
When innocence and happiness used to shower.
From hearing the doorbell and running towards the gate,
To always getting punished for reaching the school late.
Feels like yesterday, when making boats
during the rainy season we would all enjoy,
and playing in the sun without caring about getting tanned,
used to give us immense joy.
With just one chocolate,
our sad faces would turn into happy smiles
These were the simpler times.
Stories of Akbar and Birbal used to be our favourite,
From pogo to Disney, watching the amazing shows,
we all used to love it.

When everyone would be trapped in the world's chaos,
We used to rule our own lives like a boss.
How silly we thought Dora, the explorer was,
getting lost wherever she went
Little did we know that one day we would all
become like her to some extent.
Exploring our journeys, getting lost in the crowd
But always finding a way out.
Because that's what life is all about.

2. To my knights in shining armour

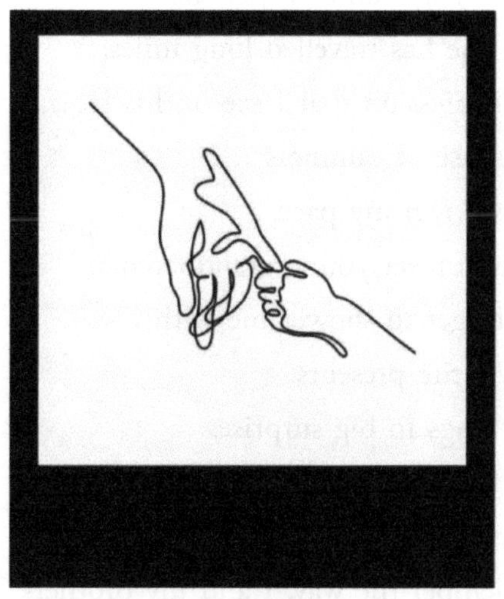

-Toast to the ones who
Have always proved to be one of the
biggest saviours and support.

Those wrinkles that embrace
her cheeks when she smiles,
Denotes those bags full of experiences
and the way she has travelled long miles.
That serene expression that I see on his face,
Gives me a sense of calmness
and it lowers down my pace.
This is to my forever young grandparents,
Who never forget to shower me with
my most favourite presents.
From little things to big surprises.
Thank you, for supporting me every time,
during any crisis.
I clearly remember the way, I and my brothers
would giggle when he bought us pastries,
We always got our solutions from them,
when our parents we needed to please.
Those bedtime stories still echo in my mind,
All those childhood moments aren't quite hard to rewind.
The way they still never fail to appreciate,
Every dish I make or every endeavour I achieve
They are the real knights in shining armour,
From whom, eternal love we will always receive.

3. School Days

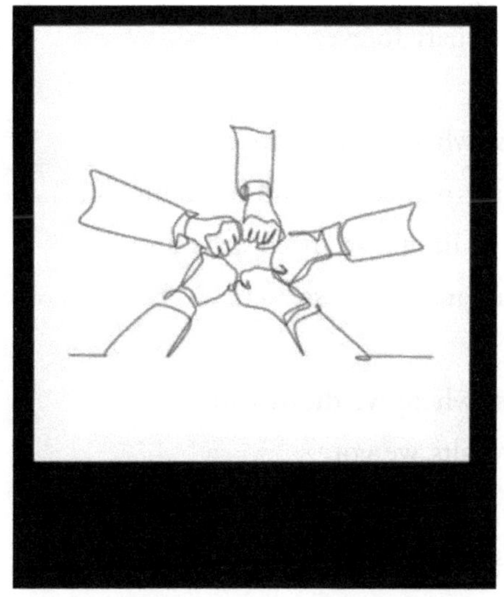

The days, whose value
we didn't realize until it was gone.
But gave us truckloads of memories
that until our lifetimes we will adorn.

School days, was a journey that began with
crying at the school gate for not leaving
mama's hand and getting in ever,
to crying at the same gate for not
wanting to depart forever.

School days, when we used to cry out loud
"I don't want to wake up and leave my bed",
pretending to have a stomach ache and
asked to stay at home instead.

School days, where we didn't care
about the results we got,
but getting two toffees on our
best friend's birthday did matter a lot.

School days, not just words but a set
of multiple emotions which went from
nonchalantly gossiping over our tiffin's together,
to wishing each other the
best for our future endeavours.

School days, a journey travelled so fast
from solving those complicated maths equations,
to give the best advice on
our friend's romantic relations.

School days were those times
when 20s music used to rule
and liking the One Direction made us look cool.

School days, where one glimpse of her crush,
would bring a hideous smile and make her cheeks blush.

School days, whose value we didn't realize until it was gone
but gave us truckloads of memories that whole lifetime we will adorn.

4. Kolkata and its charisma

-A nostalgic tour back
to the simpler times

Walking past the Bengali streets I move in awe,
When I pass through those historical red brick walls.
Feels like traveling by a time machine to the historical past,
When I revisit the Victoria Memorial and the other architectural crafts.
The city of joy never ceases to amaze
its guests with its enchanting legacy,
Portraying it through the yellow taxis
and Kolkata's delicious delicacies.
I catch a yellow taxi, wondering
how they not only carry people
but also, the city's beautiful past,
I can feel *Tagore*'s hymns still echo in the air.
Gurudev's contributions, amongst the city and people, will always last.
My day gets better when I savour the "*puchka*" and "*jhaal muri*"
for which Kolkata is famous,
For people who find joy in the little things,
it is the right place for us.
From having a walk around Park Street
to enjoy the picturesque sunset by the Ganga,
From enjoying chai in the little clay teacups
to relish the Bengali *sondesh.*
The Bengali streets are where my childhood memories
have been engraved, the ones I will always cherish.

5. To my crazy, yet sweetest siblings

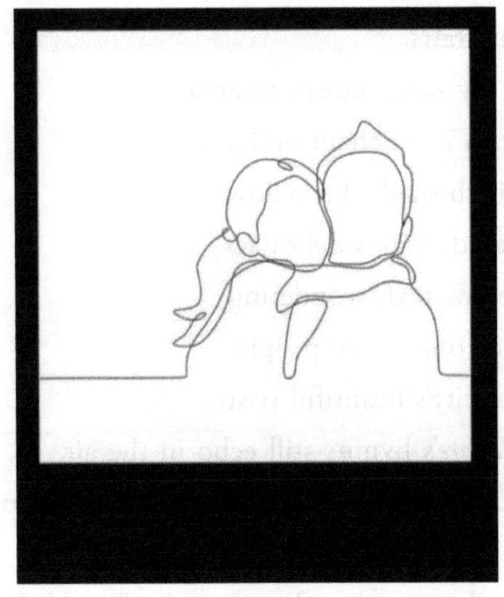

We fall, we fight
but in the end, we make things right.

We fall we fight,
But in the end, we make things right.
From being my sunshine on a cloudy day,
To enchanting me with your light in every way.

From fighting on silly things,
To handle each other's mood swings.
From keeping each other's little secrets concealed,
To keep all our big affairs unrevealed.

From annoying each other every day,
To help each other out in every way.
No matter wherever I go,
I will always love you to the core.

6. To those unforgettable friendships

-One of the biggest treasures
to be cherished.

From holding my hand whenever I needed courage,
To hear me out and remove all my baggage.
From laughing at the stupidest of moments together,
To crying narrating heartbreak stories to one another.

From the best hangouts planned at the last minute
To the Goa trips that remained unfinished.
From meeting each other every day,
To maintain long-distance friendships
in a fulfilling way.

Heartiest thank you not only to those friends
who stayed the longest,
But also, the ones who turned a few beautiful moments
into endless memories.

7. A lover's ode

A beautiful tale of how magical,
love feels for the first time.

Her eyes, as deep as the oceans
enough to drown him over.
Her smile feels warm like
the summers after the cold winter.
The flick of her hair is overwhelming,
Oh, every look,
every touch seems bewildering.
Her thoughts are striking his mind,
Whereas cupid's arrow is striking his heart.

Her absence doesn't bother,
Her Existence in his thoughts
is enough to make him fall harder.
The moon is playing peekaboo with the clouds,
Even the moonlight has lost its charm,
In front of her enchanting light in his memories.
Dark sleepless nights and stars shining,
prevailing silence itself mutters plenty of words.

8. The Night We Met

Remembering how beautiful
the night was when he looked into her eyes
for the first time.

Take me back, to "the night we met" for the first time...
Take me back to the first time when I saw you,
looking as beautiful as ever bringing life to
the gorgeous blue dress you were wearing,
the moonlight was falling on your skin
making you look angelic.
Take me back to the first time
I looked into your eyes
and said 'I love you, which I meant
from the core of my heart.
Take me back to the first time we kissed,
Your loving hands touched the back of my neck
and my fingers tenderly stroking your blushed cheeks,
it was beautifully intense and gentle.
Take me back to the first time we fought
and decided that we wouldn't talk to each other
and the next moment ended smiling and talking about love.
The night we met for the first time
will beautifully be captured in my memory forever.

“Some memories bring
us happy smiles,
and some reminds us of
people from faraway miles.”

9. Cravings and Yearnings

-When love doesn't feel
magical as it used to,
but causes deep pain inside.

Long ago there was a time,
When I could boldly call you mine.
But your love was like a butterfly,
It was beautiful but didn't stay.
Mine was like the sea that kept
flowing till it reached its shore of dismay.
There was a time when you used to smile,
And all my eyes used to do was
stare at you for a while.
But now my world without you
is like a forest without trees,
A sky without clouds and
winter without the cold breeze.
Just like the sky whose stars have died,
All I feel is an emptiness inside.
The warmth in your smile and
the spark in your eyes is all I'm craving,
I wish you would come back
to help me get over this longing.

"Sometimes we lose
and find ourselves
in the same person."

10. Reminiscences

Somethings can't be cured,
it always remains secluded
in the deep corners of our hearts.

There are times when I reminisce
us sitting together,
Planning about our beautiful forever.
Every time I see a happy ending
all I think is what caused my happiness
Slip away in the darkness.

Do I still love him?
Maybe I do.

but nothing will ever be the same,
He is a beautiful memory.
but sometimes remembering him causes pain,
That even time cannot tame.

11. Butterflies and Fireflies

Just like everything comes with a cost,
even loving someone comes
with its share of ups and downs.

They say when two people collide,
They are emersed in each other's thought's day and night.
Falling in love feels like firecrackers all around,
The blushing and the smiles know no bounds.
But when reality unfurls,
and the essence of the strawberry world flies,
Then the realization strikes, that there is more
to love than just butterflies and fireflies.
The idea of finding the perfect soulmate,
That doesn't mean that everything
will be like a walk on the cake.

There will be misunderstandings and fights,
There will be some dark stormy nights.
But after every quarrel and after every fight
The difficulties would fade and love would shine bright.
The remnants of the past won't be erased easily,
There will be insecurities flowing heavily.
Roadblocks and hurdles would be a part of the journey,
But there will be endless support, undeniable faith,
magical hope, and the power of never giving up
that will soothe every worry.
Lastly, love isn't something to be found or chased,
It will come to you in the most beautiful and unexpected ways.

"She came like a firefly
in my world of darkness,
lit up my world
and tamed my scars.
Made me fall in love with her
and my flaws too."

12. To my shining star

When finally, things begin to come into place,
and the butterflies seem to flutter again.

Those beautiful nights when we are together,
The stars shine brighter than ever.
This is to my goofy best friend
and my romantic partner.
To the one whom I love,
I fight and have endless laughter.
How magical it feels the way
out of everyone you'd find my heart to steal.
Honey the glitter in your eyes
when you see me around makes you look even prettier!
You have no idea how just by being there
in it, you turn my day even sunnier.
I'm in love with your every single detail,
from your Monday morning
"I don't want to leave the bed" cries
to your adorable weekend date surprise.
From your cute gestures to your quarrelsome fights,
No matter what, no matter when you will
always be an important part of my life.

13. To my treasure, I found amidst chaos

A happy ending, as they call it.

You are my harbour in the sea full of storms,
My little ray of sunshine makes me feel warm.
With you, the moments pass into days
and days into years,
You are my person, my pretty home
that lets go of all my fears.
Looking back to the uneven roads we have travelled,
I promise we have a beautiful journey to get unravelled.
Cause darling all the rough times have gone,
And now in front of us, we have a lifetime to adorn.

14. You and I are all alike

The phase creeps in, where the questions and insecurities sails in. Suddenly, the bubble around us breaks, and We start noticing our flaws more.

In snow white's story, the mirror
Placed on the wall,
Used to answer who's the fairest of them all.
You tube's favourite searches include,
Best remedies to be fair and light-hued.
From beauty ads to fairy tales,
The mistaken meaning of beautiful
Still prevails.
She was told to slather her face with
Sunscreens and fairness creams,
Wear dark-coloured clothes while going out.
But the truth was she could carry
Every pastel shade dress elegantly
Without a doubt.
We are living in the 21st century,
Yet the judging parameter of dark-skinned
Rather than the dark mind is still
Considered more worthy.
It's time everyone realizes that
A person isn't supposed to
Be judged by the colour of his/her skin,
But the beauty and intelligence that lies within.

“Let me be free”

15. Stop showering stereotypes

It's the 21st century, what does it take to finally overcome the stereotypes and live freely?

Rules and expectations were already
designed since the day she was born,
Which colour to like, what to wear and
how to talk, the lines were already drawn.
When she was a kid,
she was shown beautiful fairy tales,
Where there used to be females smitten
by the handsome males.
Where only men used to come and
save the princess in distress,
And the princesses were told that beauty
means being fair and wearing a pretty long dress.
In, school her little uniform was asked to be tamed,
But the narrow and wicked mindsets
weren't to be blamed.
When she grew a little old,
"Learn to make round chapattis", she was told.
Don't get mistaken here,
learning how to cook isn't a bad thing,
But it is not only for girls,
it is meant to be for every living being.
75 years of India's Independence but
her choices were still caged,
There were always questions asked
on her dreams that she chased.
When discrimination happened at the workplace
and he was given better opportunities than her,

She used to question "Why?",
" Male privilege " her female boss used to answer.
It's not only men whose eyes are clouded
by these stereotypes and limitations,
It's also those women,
who don't stand beside each other
but agree to be a part of the gender discrimination.
Amidst society's so-called moral code
and chauvinistic judgment,
All she asks for is to be independent.
When something wrong happens with a woman,
misogyny creeps in asking her to remain quiet
telling hurting her dignity won't be fair,
despite being served injustice and severe despair.
But don't mistake the women of the 21st century.
She's like the sun can glow, and has the power to burn.
Even the darkest times, into happy hours she could turn.

16. Men will be men

It's not only women, even men have to facethe shackles of patriarchy. How hard is it to understand?

"Masculinity", what does it mean?
Well, I say, what it doesn't mean is,
Liking blue over the pink hue.
I believe it is something that hides
underneath the tough shield,
it lies somewhere within you.

Be a " Man", the society says,
But dear society even a man
is allowed to express in his ways.
A man is a man when
he appreciates a female driver,
A man is a man even when he is not the family provider.
A man is a man when he sheds tears,
Because before being a man
he's a human who has his fears.
When his daughter leaves his home,
even a strong-hearted father cry.
Even he can't hide his emotions,
no matter how hard he tries.

"Oh! you are a man, it must be easy for you, people conceive
"No", it isn't when, because of some men,
disrespect the whole fraternity receives.
Only women are victims, isn't true,
Even men face the shackles of patriarchy too

17. It's Okay to express

Breaking the stigma related to Mental Health.

There will be times when you will
feel your life shattering into pieces,
things wouldn't turn out to be
the way you thought.
Little things will start making you
feel overwhelmed a lot.
What you love doing maybe
won't give you the same joy as before,
and many times, you will start feeling
trapped in your anger galore.
You will wish to cry out loud on some days,
And on other days the air around you
will seem to be filled with haze.
When the clock tick's midnight,
loneliness will start to embark
The clouds of anxiety will seem
to turn even the brightest days into the dark.
Those beautiful stars in the night sky
would start to fade.
On silent nights, the appalling
nightmares would invade.
And remember in those times,
It's okay;
It's okay to let your loved one's help
you gather your broken piece,
It's okay to let your tears
soak into the tissues till you

feel some of your pain release.
It's okay if at some days
you feel that nothing's in your hand,
But the truth is that the matters of your mind,
no one rather than yourself will the best understand.
It's okay to seek therapy and ask for help,
It's difficult but always the better way
to let out what you have felt.
It's okay if you feel like quitting,
But remember, the good part is always waiting.

**"A stardust soul,
stuck in the pale hues
of the disillusioned world
filled with dismay and betrayal."**

18. Women

She's said to be made of sugar, spice, and everything nice.But has to dwell around the walls of stereotypes and prejudice.

She enters into the world smiling,
Unaware of all the darkness prevailing.
Like a flower, she blooms gracefully in all the seasons,
Does things for people without any reasons.
Blossoms through the stages of childhood,
adolescence, and adulthood,
Struggles deeply, under the superiority of manhood.
Society keeps conspiring,
But her dreams keep aspiring.
Gentle and soft outside,
but deep down she knows how to fight,
Endures the look of exasperation in her mother's eyes
when she returns home late at night.
Longs to carve out a life of her own,
But she's taught to manage her home.
She's said to be made of sugar, spice, and everything nice.
But has to dwell around the walls of stereotypes and prejudice.
Smiles warmly and goes through the difficult times,
Her greatest enemies are the sick and appalling minds.
She is much more worthy than she thinks,
Is unaware of the joy she brings.

19. Good early days

Wish there was a time machine for real!

The clock struck midnight,
the bright moon was shattering its light.
While gazing at the star-laden sky
and sipping wine,
she travelled back to her memories of
when she was nine.
What a perfect world it was,
free from all the chaos.
A world where everyone was
Considerate about what others feel,
where bittersweet goodbyes didn't
cause wounds that were hard to heal.
The happy times when we believed
that everything lasted forever,
and the good things didn't
have to come to an end ever.
Back to the times when our
insecurities didn't clutch us tight,
and our parents would always
be aware of our plight.
But now it seems that a stardust soul
has entered into this disillusioned
world, where with time it's reality
and prejudices unfurl.

20. You call yourself ugly, but the truth is…

A poem that will remind you how beautiful you are, inside and out.

You call yourself ugly, but the truth is
that you are extremely beautiful in so many ways.

You call yourself ugly, but the truth is
you haven't seen that charming smile on your face
Your blushing cheeks when you see your favourite person,
Or that curve on your face
when your favourite food is served in.

You call yourself ugly but the truth is,
You haven't seen the lustre in your eyes
The way it shines when you talk
about how high you want to rise.

You call yourself ugly but the truth is,
You haven't seen yourself fighting
fearlessly for what's right
When you feel empowered,
you look so beautiful and bright,

You call yourself ugly but the truth is,
it's easy to notice your flaws because
the world highlights them for you,
but beauty is not only on the outside,
it is also defined as what lies within too.

21. Nature's astounding beauty

Though life is filled with hurdles and insecurities, along with that there is an abundance of beautiful things to enjoy and explore. The setting of the sun, the majestic mountains, and the cold breeze, what a bliss it feels.

The gentle breeze softly blew,
The solemn trees were standing in their queue.
It was the time for the sun to rise,
Pretty colours were lingering all over the skies.
Sunlight began to fall on the untamed river making it shine,
Its beauty sent a sensation of calmness down my spine.
The flowers were blooming around the corner,
Its petals were nodding swiftly in nature's honour.
Butterflies were fluttering all around,
Lush green grass was growing on the ground.
Now, the time had arrived for the sun to set,
The pretty birds were returning to their nests.
The view of the sunset left me enraptured,
A beautiful picture of the sky I captured.
Now it was time,
For the cold moon to shine.
The twinkling light of the stars,
was beaming in the dark.
All the elements seemed to be eternal,
The exhilarating peace in the air was simply magical.

22. Colours of the rainbow

In nature's every element, deep meanings are hidden.

The rainbow's pretty colourful hues,
Reminds me of the pretty shades
Of life from ambers to blues.
The contradictory colour of the rose,
Love, desire, and violence denote.
The lush green shade
Stands for nature's eternal beauty that never fades.
The optimistic colour of yellow,
Stands for the sun's golden glow.
The sober shade of blue
Known to be the most peaceful hue.
Orange's enthusiastic tint
Stands for energy and excitement.
Violet's royal hue is for beauty, wealth, and more
Depicts the Union of body and soul
Indigo stands for third eye and intuition
Along with impartiality, justice, and devotion.

23. Soar up high

How surprising it is, the way rain imparts joy to every living thing around.

Drops of rain falling on my face,
Enchanting my soul in numerous ways.
Finding solace in nature's bliss,
The clouds above blow down a kiss.
Branches of the trees danced joyfully in the windy breeze.
Feels like along with time,
everything around has come to a freeze.
Nature's euphoric beauty and
The blowing wind,
Bringing back my thoughts in constant rewind.
Closing my eyes and taking a deep sigh,
Wishing one day, to soar up high in the blue sky.
Isn't it lovely, the way nature never ceases
to amaze me with its beauty?
Always acting as the epitome of peace and tranquillity.

24. Twilight

The different shades of nature.

The sun is embarking on its journey
back home, after shining all-day
in the shades of yellow chrome.
Time has come,
for the vivid golden hour to bid goodbye,
And twilight to spread its
euphoric beauty and tranquillity up high.
Pretty hues are lingering over
the sky's eternal canvas,
The serene atmosphere is taking away
all the worries and soothes us.
The birds have returned to their dwellings
after the long plight,
The tulips have closed their petals
until the next sunlight.
Looking at the surreal view
of the departing day,
Gives me endless joy in a fulfilling way.

25. Snow falling on my feet

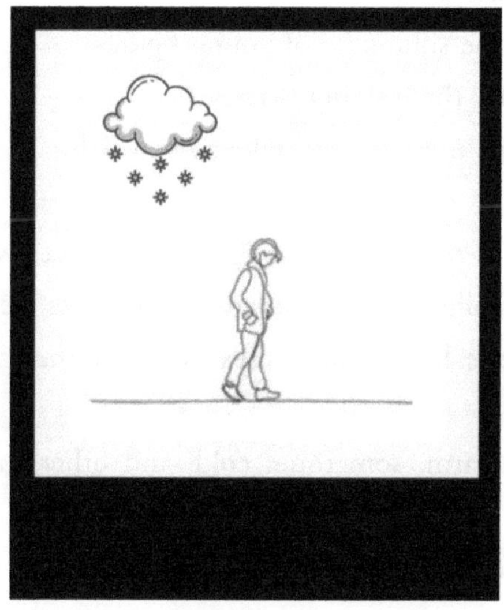

While the slushing snow falls on the ground, some realizations strike about life decisions promises and more.

The darkest evenings and longest nights have arrived,
All the moisture has departed and our skins have dried.
I feel the slushing snowfall on my feet,
As I walk past the roads of concrete.
Looking at the silhouette of young figures
playing under the evening sky,
I think about my days and take a deep sigh.

At the end of the day, it's all about the choices we make,
The responsibilities we keep and the promises we break.
Because life is like nature's seasons, never the same all the time.
Sometimes warm, sometimes cold, and other times full of storms,
but even after cold bitter winters, again the sun shines.

26. Kashmir

A piece that briefly describes the charm of heaven on earth.

High up in the north of our incredible India,
exists a heavenly place called Kashmir.
Its enchanting beauty never ceases to amaze me.
The beauty of the valley is astonishing,
The beauty of the mountains is mesmerizing,
The beauty of the forests adds to its grandeur,
Alas, the beauty of this place is the cause of my euphoria
Several rivers originate from here looking surreal
when the beams of sunlight touch its smooth surface,
The air is filled with tranquillity,
The land is filled with serenity
The enchanting environment has a fragrance of divine spirituality.
A home for all humans and religions
But inside these green and cheerful valleys,
there are dark conspiracies hidden,
and the people here just wish for their freedom and peace.

27. Hope

Hope is an invisible thread that connects everything.

Every shower of rain doesn't promise a rainbow,
Just like life doesn't always promise a happy tomorrow.
Sometimes rain brings along,
Lightning and storm.
But after every dark stormy night
A new day begins with fresh sunlight.
So as in life, some days bring along difficult times.
But these don't last forever,
good times are too awaiting to shine.
Every day is a new experience,
Bad ones are to be handled with patience.
Good ones are to have rejoiced,
In the end, life is a journey to be enjoyed.

"Sometimes, all you need to do is sit back and stop chasing the things you don't want to be away from. What is yours will find you."

28. Comebacks in life

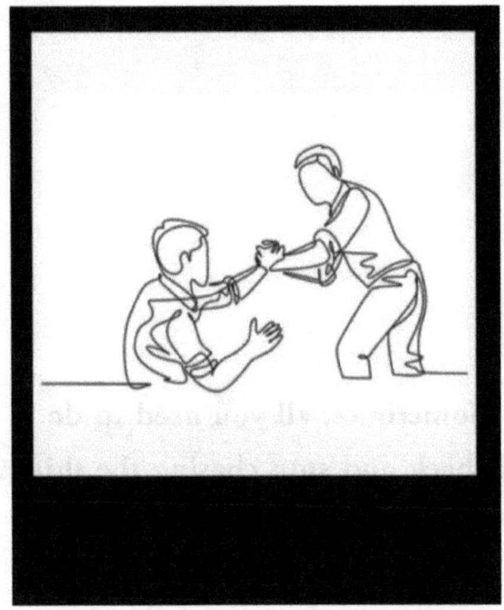

It's not the failures or setbacks that matter.
It's how you rise again that defines you.

Sometimes in life, we stumble, we trip,
We fall and we slip.
There are failures and there are setbacks,
But life is all about the lightning comebacks.
The circumstances aren't always fair,
At times leading to agony and despair,
It feels like the mind has lost its sight,
And you weren't prepared for the plight.
Even the brave soul of yours,
Deep down great pain it endures.
But as always, the darkest hour is meant to fade,
And the sun is ready to shine again in its brightest shade.
It's not important that you failed,
It made you stronger,
the path of difficulties that you trailed.
With a little more confidence and determination,
it's now time to fight back.
The world is waiting with open arms
to welcome your comeback.

29. One day at a time

It's always important,
to take a pause and breathe in.

The clock is ticking and the sun is setting again,
Life keeps passing and the journey gets mundane.
So much to achieve, so much to thrive for,
so many places and people to explore.
The chase to reach every destination continues,
and in that, we forget to enjoy the surrounding's pretty hues.
Be it meeting deadlines or maintaining relationships,
We wish to sail at once on all the ships.
To run ahead in the rat race,
We want to solve everything in haste.

How hard is it to understand,
that just like a tangled wire can't be sorted in one go
All our problems, together we can't blow!
The roadblocks and hurdles will keep coming
in your way because that's what life is about
It's not the big endeavours or the small failures,
But the journey that is to be enjoyed throughout.

30. A train journey

Comparing life to a train journey.

Life is like a train journey,
Sometimes the train delays
in reaching the stations,
On the other hand,
some stations are reached
unexpectedly before time.
Some passengers come and leave too soon,
And some stay with us till the end.
Similarly in life,
sometimes good things take time
And sometimes they come to us
Unexpectedly before time.
A lot of people come and leave,
but there are those too
who stay, till the end destination.

31. Falling in love

A reminder to be grateful for what you have and till you have!

I have started to fall in love with each hour I pass,
Each moment I spare and each day I spend.
Because I have understood that life
is no less than a maths equation,
Where on balance, all the sides depend.
An equation where joy and happiness are to be added
And the stress and negativity to be subtracted.
But one thing that applies everywhere is
that nothing is to be taken for granted.
Spending blurry nights, bright days,
and chasing the unfinished dreams,
I am starting to fall in love with everything.
No one knows, how many days we are left with to count,
But what I know is, I don't want to spend them in worry and doubt.
So always bet on yourself and take some chances,
Because you never know what your last moment is.

Author's Bio

Raashi is a young writer and poet, who finds her solace in books and music. She loves to communicate her thoughts and aspires to become someone capable to leave a positive mark on the minds of people. She has embarked on her journey as an author by launching her debut book and she wishes you a happy read!

9 798885 911856

Printed by Libri Plureos GmbH in Hamburg, Germany